LEAVING THE MATRIX

Title: Leaving the Matrix: The 9-to-5 Scam and Building Generational Wealth Through Digital Products and E-books

Table of Contents

1. Introduction
   2. Understanding the 9-to-5 Mindset
      - The Illusion of Job Security
      - Limitations of Traditional Income
   3. Identifying the Matrix
      - The Systematic Barriers to Wealth
      - The Role of Consumerism
   4. The Case for Digital Products
      - Low Overhead and High Scalability
      - Infinite Shelf Life and Global Reach
      - Flexibility and Autonomy
   5. The E-book Revolution
      - The Rise of Self-Publishing
      - Niche Markets and Target Audiences
      - Strategies for Successful E-book Creation
   6. Steps to Transition from Employee to Entrepreneur
      - Skills Assessment and Development
      - Building a Personal Brand
      - Creating and Launching Your First Digital Product
   7. Marketing Your Digital Products
      - Understanding Your Audience
      - Utilizing Social Media and Content Marketing
      - Leveraging SEO and Email Marketing
   8. Building Multiple Streams of Income
      - Expanding Your Offerings
      - Affiliate Marketing and Online Courses
      - Subscription Models and Membership Sites
   9. Maintaining Financial Stability
      - Budgeting for Entrepreneurs

        - Emergency Funds and Investments
        - Reinvesting in Your Business
   10. Cultivating a Wealth-Building Mindset
        - Overcoming Fear and Doubt
        - Continuous Learning and Adaptation
        - Long-term Vision for Generational Wealth
   11. Real-Life Case Studies
        - Success Stories of Digital Entrepreneurs
        - Lessons Learned and Best Practices
   12. Conclusion
   13. Resources
        - Recommended Tools and Platforms
        - Further Reading and Learning Opportunities

Chapter 1: Introduction

The traditional 9-to-5 job has long been viewed as a stable pathway to financial security. However, the realities of modern economics demonstrate that this model often falls short of delivering true wealth and freedom. "Leaving the Matrix" delves into the essence of breaking free from this entrenched mindset and embraces the potential of digital products and e-books as viable means for building generational wealth.

"Leaving the Matrix" explores how this entrenched 9-to-5 mindset can keep individuals trapped in a cycle of limited income and lack of control over their time and destiny. While once considered the most reliable way to achieve financial security, the modern economy has introduced more flexible and scalable opportunities, particularly through digital products and e-books.

In this book, we'll uncover how leveraging these digital tools can help you break free from the conventional working model. Whether you're looking to create passive income or scale a business, embracing the digital economy opens doors to generational wealth and the freedom to live life on your own terms. You no longer have to exchange time for money; by creating and selling digital assets, you can establish multiple streams of income, allowing for both financial growth and personal freedom.

In this chapter, we'll begin by understanding the limitations of the 9-to-5 system and why more people are choosing to leave this traditional structure behind. Then, we'll introduce the power of digital products—like e-books, online courses, and digital tools—as key components in the journey toward financial independence.

Chapter 2: Understanding the 9-to-5 Mindset

While a steady paycheck provides comfort, it often comes at the expense of personal freedom and wealth accumulation. Job security fosters complacency, which can limit creativity and risk-taking essential for entrepreneurial success.

"Understanding the 9-to-5 Mindset" refers to exploring the conventional mentality and lifestyle associated with working a traditional job where people follow set hours, typically from 9 AM to 5 PM. This mindset often involves:

1. Structured Routine: People with a 9-to-5 mindset typically expect a fixed daily routine, with clear boundaries between work hours and personal time.
2. Job Security and Stability: Many individuals seek the stability of a full-time job, where income and benefits are predictable and consistent.
3. Work-Life Balance: There is often a strong emphasis on maintaining separation between work and personal life, with weekends and evenings reserved for rest and family.
4. Career Progression: In this mindset, individuals often follow

a linear career path, moving up within a company through promotions and raises, valuing long-term job security.

Understanding this mindset can help entrepreneurs or those pursuing non-traditional careers, such as freelancing or starting a business, identify the appeal of the 9-to-5 model and recognize the shifts needed in mentality when moving to more flexible, self-driven career paths.

Chapter 3: Identifying the Matrix

The societal constructs of success, such as consumerism and debt, create barriers to true wealth. Recognizing these barriers is the first step toward escaping the matrix of traditional employment.

"Identifying the Matrix" could refer to recognizing the systems, structures, and patterns that shape our lives, especially in terms of work, society, or personal development. In the context of mindset or career, it often means:

1. Breaking Out of Societal Norms: The "Matrix" can symbolize the conventional expectations placed on individuals, such as the traditional path of education, career, and retirement. Identifying it involves becoming aware of these societal constructs and questioning whether they align with your personal values and goals.
2. Recognizing Limiting Beliefs: Many people operate within mental frameworks that limit their potential. These beliefs—often ingrained by society, family, or culture—can be seen as part of the "Matrix" that keeps people from pursuing unconventional paths like entrepreneurship, creative careers, or other fulfilling life choices.
3. Awareness of Control Mechanisms: The Matrix can also represent systems of control—such as financial dependencies, consumerism, or job security—that may hold people in place, making them feel stuck or unable to pursue more independent or purpose-driven paths.

In essence, "Identifying the Matrix" is about recognizing the invisible forces that shape behavior, thoughts, and life decisions, and finding ways to step outside of them to pursue a more authentic, self-determined life.

Chapter 4: The Case for Digital Products

Digital products offer remarkable benefits: they require minimal upfront investment, can reach global audiences, and provide passive income potential. Exploring these benefits reveals opportunities for significant financial growth.

"The Case for Digital Products" highlights the advantages of creating and selling digital goods, particularly in today's increasingly online marketplace. Here are some key reasons why digital products are compelling:

1. Low Overhead Costs: Digital products like eBooks, courses, software, and printables don't require physical materials, shipping, or warehousing. Once created, they can be sold an infinite number of times without extra production costs.
2. Scalability: Unlike physical products, digital goods can be distributed globally with minimal effort. This makes it easy to scale, allowing entrepreneurs to grow their businesses quickly without the logistical challenges of manufacturing or inventory.
3. Passive Income: Digital products can generate passive income. After the initial creation, they can be sold repeatedly, providing a revenue stream without constant active involvement.
4. Flexibility and Customization: Digital products offer endless possibilities for customization. They can be updated, revised, or improved over time without incurring significant costs, allowing businesses to stay relevant and meet customer demands easily.
5. Global Reach: Selling digital products online removes geographic limitations, giving entrepreneurs access to a worldwide customer base. This reach allows businesses to tap into diverse

markets and grow quickly.

6. Eco-friendly: Digital products are environmentally friendly as they don't require packaging, shipping, or physical resources. This makes them attractive to consumers who value sustainability.

In summary, digital products present an appealing business model because of their low cost, scalability, potential for passive income, and ability to reach a global audience, making them a powerful choice for entrepreneurs in today's digital age.

Chapter 5: The E-book Revolution

E-books have democratized publishing, allowing anyone to share knowledge. Identifying niche markets and effectively targeting audiences are crucial for standing out in a saturated market.

"The E-book Revolution" refers to the dramatic shift in the publishing industry brought about by the rise of digital books, transforming how people consume literature and how authors and publishers distribute content. Key aspects of this revolution include:

1. Accessibility: E-books can be instantly downloaded and accessed on a variety of devices like smartphones, tablets, and e-readers, making reading more convenient and accessible to people globally. This convenience has led to widespread adoption.
2. Democratization of Publishing: The rise of self-publishing platforms like Amazon Kindle Direct Publishing (KDP) has empowered independent authors to publish and distribute their work without the need for traditional publishing houses. This has created opportunities for more voices to be heard and stories to be told.
3. Lower Production Costs: Compared to print books, e-books eliminate the costs associated with printing, shipping, and storing physical copies. This has made publishing more affordable for authors and publishers, leading to a wider variety of books being available.
4. Ease of Distribution: With e-books, distribution is instanta-

neous and global. Authors can reach a worldwide audience with minimal effort, giving them the ability to grow their readership more quickly than with traditional print books.

5. Interactive Features: E-books often come with enhanced features such as hyperlinks, multimedia, or interactive elements that traditional print books cannot offer, enhancing the reader's experience.

6. Changing Reading Habits: The e-book revolution has changed how people read. Many prefer the portability and customization features (such as adjustable font size and background color) that e-readers and apps offer, allowing for a more personalized reading experience.

In summary, the e-book revolution has transformed the publishing landscape by making reading more accessible, enabling authors to self-publish, reducing costs, and offering a global platform for content distribution. It has opened up opportunities for both readers and writers, reshaping how stories are shared in the digital age.

Chapter 6: Steps to Transition from Employee to Entrepreneur

Aspiring entrepreneurs must assess their skills, build a personal brand, and determine their first product offering. This transition requires careful planning and execution.

Transitioning from an employee to an entrepreneur requires careful planning, mindset shifts, and strategic actions. Here are key steps to guide this transition:

1. Develop a Clear Vision:
- Start by defining your business idea and vision. Consider what kind of business you want to build and why. Understanding your passion, strengths, and market opportunities is crucial in setting the right foundation.
2. Build Financial Security:
- Before leaving your job, create a financial safety net. This includes saving at least 6–12 months of living expenses and startup

capital to support your business during the early stages, as most businesses take time to become profitable.

3. Start as a Side Hustle:
- If possible, begin your entrepreneurial journey as a side hustle while keeping your full-time job. This allows you to test your business idea, gain experience, and build initial revenue without the financial pressure of full-time entrepreneurship.

4. Develop a Business Plan:
- Create a solid business plan that outlines your business goals, target audience, marketing strategies, revenue model, and financial projections. This will help you stay focused and organized while attracting potential investors or partners.

5. Grow Your Network:
- Networking is essential for any entrepreneur. Start building relationships with mentors, industry professionals, potential customers, and other entrepreneurs. This network can provide guidance, feedback, and valuable connections to help you grow your business.

6. Acquire Relevant Skills:
- As an entrepreneur, you may need skills that differ from those required in your current job. Invest time in learning about marketing, sales, finance, and other areas relevant to running a business. Online courses, books, and mentorship can help you acquire the necessary knowledge.

7. Test Your Product or Service:
- Before fully committing, test your product or service in the market to gather feedback. You can start with a minimum viable product (MVP) or conduct pilot programs. This will help you validate your business idea and make necessary improvements before scaling.

8. Set a Transition Date:
- Decide on a specific date when you'll fully transition from your job to your business. Having a timeline gives you a clear focus and sense of urgency, but make sure it aligns with your financial readiness and business progress.

9. Leave Your Job Professionally:
- When you're ready to make the leap, leave your job on

good terms. Give appropriate notice, complete your responsibilities, and maintain professional relationships. These connections could be valuable to your business down the road.

10. Fully Commit to Your Business:
- Once you make the transition, fully commit to your business and adopt an entrepreneurial mindset. This involves embracing risk, taking ownership of decisions, and being willing to adapt as challenges arise. Stay focused, resilient, and open to learning from both successes and failures.

By following these steps, you can transition from employee to entrepreneur strategically, minimizing risks and increasing your chances of success.

Chapter 7: Marketing Your Digital Products

A thorough understanding of your target market is vital. Effective marketing strategies, including content marketing and social media outreach, can drive sales and establish authority in your niche.

Marketing digital products effectively requires a blend of online strategies to reach the right audience and drive sales. Here are key steps to market your digital products successfully:

Marketing Your Digital Products:

1. Identify Your Audience: Know your target customers (demographics, interests, pain points) to tailor your messaging and choose the right platforms.
2. Create a Value Proposition: Clearly communicate how your product solves a problem or adds value, and highlight what sets it apart.
3. Build an Online Presence: Develop a professional website or landing page with product info, testimonials, and strong calls-to-

action.

4. Leverage Social Media: Use platforms like Instagram, Facebook, and LinkedIn to share updates and run targeted ads.

5. Build an Email List: Offer free content to grow your list, and send newsletters with updates, promotions, and tips.

6. Use Content Marketing: Create videos, webinars, and guest on podcasts to educate and engage your audience.

7. Collaborate with Influencers: Partner with influencers or set up an affiliate program to expand your reach.

8. Run Paid Ads: Use Google, Facebook, and retargeting ads to drive traffic and re-engage potential buyers.

9. Offer Discounts or Bundles: Encourage quick purchases with limited-time offers or early-bird discounts.

10. Showcase Testimonials: Build trust by featuring customer reviews and case studies on your site and social media.

11. Utilize SEO: Optimize your site for relevant keywords to drive organic traffic.

12. Offer Free Trials: For software or subscriptions, free trials can help build trust and allow users to try before buying.

13. Sell on Marketplaces: Use platforms like Etsy, Udemy, or Amazon to reach a wider audience.

By implementing these strategies, you can effectively market your digital products and grow your business.

Chapter 8: Building Multiple Streams of Income

Diversity in income sources enhances financial resilience. Exploring affiliate marketing, online courses, and subscription services can provide additional revenue and stability.

Building multiple streams of income is a strategic approach to diversify your earnings and create financial stability. Here are key steps to help you develop multiple income sources effectively:

1. Assess Your Skills and Interests

- Start by evaluating your skills, interests, and expertise. Identify areas where you have knowledge or passion, as this will make it easier to create and sustain additional income streams.

2. Create Passive Income Sources

- Investments: Consider investing in stocks, bonds, real estate, or mutual funds that can generate dividends or rental income.
- Digital Products: Develop eBooks, online courses, or downloadable templates that can be sold repeatedly without ongoing effort.
- Affiliate Marketing: Promote products or services through your website, blog, or social media, earning commissions for each sale made through your referral links.

3. Start a Side Business

- Launch a side business that aligns with your skills or interests. This could include freelance work, consulting, or offering services like graphic design, writing, or coaching. Starting small allows you to test the waters without a huge upfront commitment.

4. Leverage Existing Assets

- If you have assets such as a spare room, consider renting it out on platforms like Airbnb. If you own equipment or tools, think about renting them out for extra income.
- Create a YouTube channel or a blog based on your expertise or hobbies and monetize it through ads, sponsorships, or merchandise.

5. Explore Gig Economy Opportunities

- Participate in gig economy platforms like Uber, Lyft, or TaskRabbit, where you can offer services or transportation on a flexible schedule. This allows you to earn extra income on top of your regular job.

6. Invest in Real Estate

- Real estate can be a lucrative source of income. Consider purchasing rental properties, engaging in house flipping, or investing in real estate investment trusts (REITs) to earn passive income through rent or property appreciation.

7. Create a Subscription Model

- If you have a product or service that can be delivered regularly, consider establishing a subscription model. This could apply to anything from monthly curated boxes, online memberships, or exclusive content access.

8. Automate and Delegate

- As your income streams grow, look for ways to automate processes or delegate tasks. For example, using tools for email marketing, social media scheduling, and customer service can save you time and effort.

9. Continue Learning and Adapting

- Stay informed about market trends and new opportunities. Attend workshops, take courses, and network with others to learn from their experiences and find inspiration for new income streams.

10. Monitor and Evaluate Your Income Streams

- Regularly assess the performance of your income sources. Identify which streams are most profitable and which may need adjustment or improvement. This allows you to focus your efforts on the most effective strategies.

11. Maintain a Balanced Approach

- While building multiple streams of income is beneficial, ensure you don't

Chapter 9: Maintaining Financial Stability

Setting a budget, maintaining an emergency fund, and reinvesting profits are foundational practices for sustained business health. Financial literacy is critical for long-term success.

Maintaining financial stability is essential for personal well-being and long-term security. It involves managing your finances effectively to ensure that you can meet your obligations, save for the future, and achieve your financial goals. Here are key strategies to help you maintain financial stability:

1. Create a Budget

- Track Income and Expenses: Keep a detailed record of your income and expenditures to understand where your money goes.
- Set Spending Limits: Establish limits for different categories (e.g., groceries, entertainment, savings) to prevent overspending.
- Adjust Regularly: Review and adjust your budget regularly based on changing circumstances or financial goals.

2. Build an Emergency Fund

- Aim for 3-6 Months of Expenses: Save enough to cover at least three to six months' worth of living expenses. This provides a safety net in case of job loss, medical emergencies, or unexpected expenses.
- Keep It Accessible: Store your emergency fund in a high-yield savings account to earn interest while keeping it easily accessible.

3. Manage Debt Wisely

- Prioritize Payments: Focus on paying off high-interest debt first, such as credit cards, while making minimum payments on other debts.
- Avoid New Debt: Be cautious about taking on new debt, especially for non-essential items. Stick to your budget and consider using cash for purchases to avoid impulse buying.
- Consider Consolidation: If you have multiple debts, consider consolidating them into a single loan with a lower interest rate.

4. Invest for the Future

- Retirement Accounts: Contribute to retirement accounts like a 401(k) or IRA to benefit from tax advantages and employer matches if available.
- Diversify Investments: Consider a mix of stocks, bonds, and other investment vehicles to balance risk and return.
- Stay Informed: Continuously educate yourself about investment options and market trends to make informed decisions.

5. Increase Your Income

- Seek Raises or Promotions: Negotiate for salary increases at your current job or look for advancement opportunities.
- Develop New Skills: Invest in education or training to enhance your skills and increase your value in the job market.
- Create Additional Income Streams: Consider side hustles, freelance work, or passive income opportunities such as rental properties or investments.

6. Plan for Large Expenses

- Save in Advance: If you anticipate significant expenses (e.g., a car purchase, home repairs, or education), start saving early to avoid financial strain.

- Set Up Dedicated Funds: Create separate savings accounts for specific goals to help you stay organized and focused.

7. Review and Adjust Regularly

- Monitor Financial Health: Regularly review your financial statements, investments, and budget to assess your financial health and make necessary adjustments.
- Set Goals: Establish short-term and long-term financial goals, and track your progress towards achieving them.

8. Seek Professional Advice

- Consult Financial Advisors: If you're unsure about investment strategies or financial planning, consider seeking advice from certified financial planners or advisors.
- Educate Yourself: Read books, attend workshops, or take courses on personal finance and investing to improve your knowledge and skills.

9. Practice Financial Discipline

- Live Within Your Means: Avoid lifestyle inflation and unnecessary expenses. Focus on essential needs and long-term goals.
- Be Mindful of Spending Triggers: Identify what drives your spending habits and take steps to mitigate impulse purchases or emotional spending.

10. Stay Adaptable

- Adjust to Changes: Be prepared to adapt your financial strategy in response to life changes such as job loss, unexpected expenses, or changes in income.
- Stay Informed About Financial Trends: Keep an eye on economic conditions, interest rates, and market trends that may affect your financial stability.

By implementing these strategies, you can maintain financial stability, protect yourself against uncertainties, and work towards achieving your long-term financial goals.

Chapter 10: Cultivating a Wealth-Building Mindset

Success is significantly influenced by mindset. Overcoming self-doubt and embracing a culture of continuous learning prepare individuals for the challenges of entrepreneurship.

Here's a more concise version of Cultivating a Wealth-Building Mindset:

Cultivating a Wealth-Building Mindset

1. Shift Your Perspective on Money

- View money as a tool for achieving goals, embracing an abundance mindset instead of scarcity.

2. Set Clear Financial Goals

- Establish specific, measurable goals (SMART) and visualize your desired outcomes to motivate action.

3. Educate Yourself

- Invest in financial literacy through books, courses, and reputable resources to empower informed decisions.

4. Adopt a Growth Mindset

- Embrace challenges as learning opportunities and seek continuous improvement in skills and knowledge.

5. Practice Discipline and Consistency

- Create and stick to a budget, and automate savings and investments for consistent wealth-building.

6. Surround Yourself with Positive Influences

- Build a network of like-minded individuals and seek mentorship from those who have achieved financial success.

7. Cultivate Gratitude

- Practice gratitude for your current situation and avoid comparisons with others to maintain a positive outlook.

8. Take Calculated Risks

- Be open to opportunities that involve risks, but analyze potential rewards before making financial decisions.

9. Focus on Value Creation

- Create value for others through your work or investments, which can lead to financial rewards.

10. Review and Adjust Regularly

- Monitor your financial progress and be flexible in adapting your strategies as needed.

By adopting these principles, you can foster a mindset conducive to financial growth and stability.

Chapter 11: Real-Life Case Studies

The journey of successful digital entrepreneurs illustrates the application of strategies discussed throughout this manuscript. Insights from their experiences can guide new entrepreneurs in avoiding common pitfalls.

Here's a more concise version of Real-Life Case Studies focused on cultivating a wealth-building mindset:

Real-Life Case Studies

1. Elon Musk
   • Overview: Founder of Tesla and SpaceX, Musk transitioned from software to electric cars and space exploration.
   • Takeaway: Embraces calculated risks and a growth mindset, constantly solving complex problems.
2. Oprah Winfrey
   • Overview: From a challenging childhood to a media empire, Oprah transformed her passion for storytelling into success.
   • Takeaway: Focuses on clear goals and creating value, using her platform for positive change.
3. Warren Buffett
   • Overview: A renowned investor and CEO of Berkshire Hathaway, Buffett emphasizes disciplined investing.
   • Takeaway: Stresses financial education and long-term thinking, seeking intrinsic value over quick gains.
4. Sara Blakely
   • Overview: Founder of Spanx, Blakely turned a $5,000 investment into a billion-dollar company.
   • Takeaway: Demonstrates resilience and creativity, embracing failure as part of the journey.
5. Richard Branson
   • Overview: Founder of the Virgin Group, Branson diversified across multiple industries.
   • Takeaway: Highlights the importance of pursuing passions and creating products that serve customers.
6. Jessica Alba

- Overview: Co-founder of The Honest Company, focused on non-toxic products for families.
- Takeaway: Identified a market gap and built a trusted brand based on transparency.

7. Pat Flynn
- Overview: Built a successful online business after being laid off, focusing on passive income.
- Takeaway: Shares knowledge and builds community, creating diverse income streams.

These case studies illustrate how individuals exemplify a wealth-building mindset through calculated risks, resilience, and a focus on value creation.

Chapter 12: Conclusion

Leaving the matrix and the conventional 9-to-5 structure opens avenues for wealth that transcend generations. Commitment, strategic planning, and a willingness to adapt are crucial for achieving this goal.

Escape the 9-5 Matrix: Unlock Freedom with E-books and Digital Products

Tired of the daily grind and the limitations of the traditional 9-5? It's time to break free from the matrix of the corporate world and create a life of independence, flexibility, and financial freedom. This book reveals how you can escape the outdated system designed to keep you stuck in a never-ending cycle, and shows you how to leverage the power of e-books and digital products to create a scalable, passive income stream.

You'll discover the strategies successful entrepreneurs use to build profitable online businesses by monetizing their knowledge, creativity, and expertise through digital content. Whether you want to write your own e-book, create an online course, or sell unique digital products, this guide will provide you with actionable steps to launch, market, and grow your digital empire.

Learn how to:

- Identify profitable niches and create valuable content
- Build a loyal audience and turn them into paying customers
- Market and sell your e-books and digital products effectively
- Scale your online business to achieve long-term success

Say goodbye to the 9-5 scam and hello to a life of freedom, where your time is yours to design. It's time to take control of your future—embrace the digital revolution and start living on your own terms.

Leaving the 9-to-5 matrix is important for several reasons, many of which center around gaining control over your time, financial independence, and living a more fulfilling life. Here are a few key reasons why breaking free from the traditional work model is so crucial:

1. Time Freedom

One of the greatest limitations of the 9-to-5 system is that it consumes the majority of your day, leaving little time for personal growth, creativity, and family. By escaping this structure, you regain control over your time, allowing you to prioritize what matters most in your life. This can lead to a better work-life balance and the ability to live life on your terms.

2. Financial Independence

Traditional jobs often come with capped salaries, no matter how hard you work. When you leave the 9-to-5, particularly by creating your own business or investing in digital products, you have the potential for unlimited income. This financial independence gives you the freedom to live more comfortably and take control of your financial future, rather than relying on a paycheck.

3. Escaping the Rat Race

The 9-to-5 matrix often locks people into a cycle of living paycheck to paycheck, with little opportunity for real financial growth or freedom. Many people spend decades working for someone else's dreams, only to retire and face the reality that they never truly enjoyed life. Leaving the 9-to-5 allows you to escape this race and build something that benefits you directly.

4. Flexibility and Autonomy

In a traditional job, you're bound by someone else's rules, schedule, and priorities. By leaving that behind, you gain the autonomy to make decisions that align with your own goals and values. You can work from anywhere, set your own hours, and choose the projects or businesses you want to invest your energy into. This flexibility can lead to a more satisfying and self-directed life.

5. Unlocking Creativity and Purpose

The 9-to-5 structure can stifle creativity and limit your potential. Many people feel unfulfilled, stuck in monotonous routines that don't allow them to explore their true passions or purpose. When you step outside of the corporate matrix, you have the opportunity to pursue meaningful work, explore new ventures, and channel your creativity into projects that inspire you.

6. Building Generational Wealth

By staying in the 9-to-5 system, it's challenging to accumulate significant wealth, as your income is often limited by hours worked and salary caps. However, through entrepreneurship, digital products, and investing, you have the potential to create multiple streams of income, which can lead to financial freedom and the opportunity to build generational wealth for your family.

7. Adapting to a Changing World

The workforce is changing rapidly due to advancements in technology, automation, and the rise of remote work. The 9-to-5 model is becoming outdated, and many traditional jobs are disappearing. By leaving the matrix and investing in digital skills or creating online income streams, you're positioning yourself for success in the future of work, where flexibility and innovation are key.

8. Greater Security Through Diversification

While a traditional job may seem secure, in reality, it places all your financial stability in the hands of one employer. If you lose your job, you lose your entire income source. By building a business or creating digital products, you diversify your income streams, making you less vulnerable to economic shifts or layoffs.

Conclusion

Leaving the 9-to-5 matrix is about more than just quitting a job—it's about reclaiming your time, financial future, and sense of purpose. By stepping into the world of entrepreneurship, freelancing, or digital product creation, you open the door to a more fulfilling, autonomous, and financially independent life. The sooner you make the shift, the sooner you can start living on your own terms.

In 2024, several types of digital products generated millions of dollars in revenue. Some of the top-selling categories include:

1. Online Courses and E-learning: Educational content continues to dominate, with courses in tech, business, wellness, and

creative fields like photography and design selling exceptionally well. Platforms like Udemy and Coursera, along with independent creators, capitalize on the ongoing demand for self-improvement and skills development.

2. Digital Templates and Design Assets: Ready-to-use templates for websites, presentations, social media, and email marketing are highly profitable. These products save time for businesses and individuals looking for professional design solutions, with website themes and UI kits being especially popular.

3. E-books: E-books remain a lucrative digital product, especially in niches like self-help, entrepreneurship, and niche technical topics. Authors use e-books as both direct revenue streams and lead generation tools.

4. Subscription-based Digital Libraries: Offering premium access to exclusive content, such as video tutorials, toolkits, or specialized knowledge in membership sites, has become a successful model for recurring revenue. This includes everything from creative resources to business strategies and personal development.

5. Audio and Music Products: Musicians and sound designers made millions through royalty-free music packs, sound effects, and specialized audio products for specific industries like game development and content creation.

6. Mobile Apps: Apps, especially in the productivity, wellness, and entertainment categories, remain a strong revenue generator. The global app market was projected to reach nearly $935 billion, with substantial earnings coming from both paid downloads and in-app purchases.

7. Interactive Planners and Journals: Digital planners and productivity tools designed for personal development, habit tracking, and goal setting have surged in popularity. These tools allow for customization and interactivity, driving significant sales.

These products reflect the growing demand for convenience, personalization, and tools that help users achieve their goals more efficiently. Many creators continue to innovate within these categories, expanding their reach and profit potential.

Sources: , .

Chapter 13: Resources

A carefully curated list of tools, platforms, and further reading provides invaluable support for those embarking on the journey toward financial independence through digital products and e-books.

Tools for Creating Digital Products

1. Canva: A versatile design platform perfect for creating e-books, social media graphics, and digital downloads. Canva's drag-and-drop interface and free templates make it easy for non-designers to create professional-quality content.
   - Website: www.canva.com
2. Scrivener: An ideal tool for writing e-books, Scrivener helps authors organize their research, notes, and drafts all in one place, simplifying the e-book creation process.
   - Website: www.literatureandlatte.com
3. Adobe InDesign: A powerful tool for creating well-designed e-books, digital magazines, and PDFs. Perfect for those who need more control over formatting and design.
   - Website: www.adobe.com/products/indesign.html
4. Teachable: A platform for building and selling online courses. If you plan to expand beyond e-books and want to offer educational content in different formats, Teachable is an excellent option.
   - Website: www.teachable.com
5. Google Docs: A simple and effective tool for writing and collaborating on e-books. It's free, cloud-based, and perfect for co-authoring or sharing drafts with editors.
   - Website: docs.google.com

Platforms for Selling Digital Products

1. Shopify: A leading e-commerce platform that allows you to set up an online store to sell digital products like e-books, courses, or templates. Shopify is user-friendly and integrates with various payment gateways.
   - Website: www.shopify.com
2. Gumroad: A great platform for creators to sell digital products like e-books, music, art, and more. It's easy to set up and provides a simple interface for creators to upload and sell their products directly to customers.
   - Website: www.gumroad.com
3. Etsy: Known for handmade and vintage goods, Etsy also allows sellers to offer digital downloads such as templates, designs, and digital art. It's ideal for creators who want to tap into a marketplace with an established audience.
   - Website: www.etsy.com
4. Amazon Kindle Direct Publishing (KDP): One of the best platforms for self-publishing e-books. KDP allows you to reach millions of readers through Amazon's marketplace, making it one of the most effective ways to sell your e-book.
   - Website: kdp.amazon.com

Marketing Tools

1. Mailchimp: An email marketing tool that helps you build a mailing list and communicate with your audience. Mailchimp is key for nurturing leads, promoting your digital products, and driving sales.
   - Website: www.mailchimp.com
2. Buffer: A social media management platform that allows you to schedule and manage posts across multiple platforms. Buffer can help automate the promotion of your digital products.
   - Website: www.buffer.com
3. ConvertKit: A powerful email marketing tool designed for creators, ConvertKit allows you to build a subscriber list, create automated email funnels, and sell products through email.
   - Website: www.convertkit.com

Further Reading

1. "The $100 Startup" by Chris Guillebeau: This book outlines how to start a business with minimal capital by leveraging digital products and low-cost tools.
- Available at: Amazon

2. "Dotcom Secrets" by Russell Brunson: A guide to mastering sales funnels, this book is essential for anyone looking to sell digital products online effectively.
- Available at: Amazon

3. "The Lean Startup" by Eric Ries: This book emphasizes testing and validating ideas before scaling, a must-read for creators starting a digital product business.
- Available at: Amazon

4. "Crushing It!" by Gary Vaynerchuk: A motivational guide to building a personal brand and leveraging social media to sell products, including digital ones.
- Available at: Amazon

Conclusion

These resources are just the beginning of your journey toward financial independence through digital products and e-books. As you explore and implement these tools, keep experimenting and refining your approach to ensure success. With the right tools and strategies, the digital economy offers limitless potential.

This manuscript outlines a roadmap for individuals seeking to redefine their approach to wealth creation, moving beyond traditional employment and into the dynamic world of digital entrepreneurship.

www.ingramcontent.com/pod-product-compliance
Lightning Source LLC
Chambersburg PA
CBHW071001220526
45471CB00007B/3124